by Martha Wisdom North   Illustrated by Tanya Maneki

CHILDREN, CHILDREN,
What is True?

Jesus loves you
and I do too.
♡ Martha

"Dedicate your children to God and point them
in the way that they should go, and the values
they've learned from you will be with them for life."
Proverbs 22.6 TPT

Adam, Adam,
what is true?

God made the world,
for me and for you.

GENESIS 1-2

God kept His promise,
to me and to you.

GENESIS 6-9

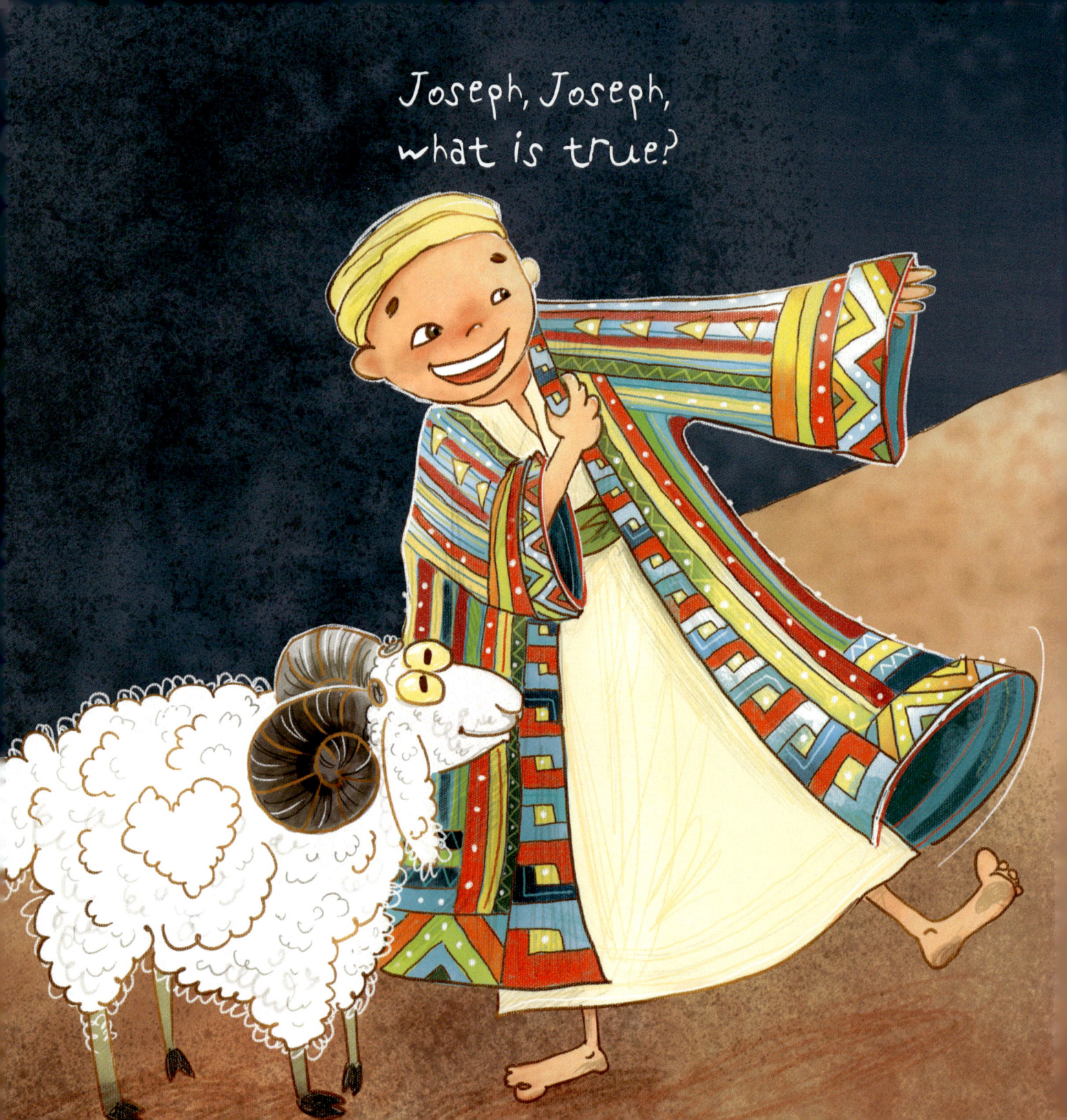

Joseph, Joseph,
what is true?

God had a plan,
for me and for you.

GENESIS 37, 39-47

Moses, Moses,
what is true?

God set a path,
for me and for you.

Exodus 13-14, 19-20

God made a way,
for me and for you.

Joshua 6

God heard the cry,
from me and from you.

1 Samuel 1-2:11

Samuel, Samuel,
what is true?

God reached out,
to me and to you.

1 Samuel 3

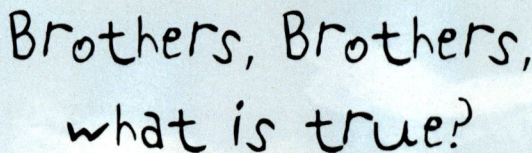

Brothers, Brothers,
what is true?

God saw the heart,
of me and of you.

1 Samuel 16:1-13

God won the battle,
for me and for you.

1 Samuel 17

Esther, Esther,
what is true?

God gave the choice,
to me and to you.

Esther

God heard the prayer,
of me and of you.

Daniel 6

God had a message,
for me and for you.

Jonah 1-4

God sent a Savior,
for me and for you.

Luke 2:8-20

Fishermen, Fishermen,
what is true?

Jesus said "Follow",
to me and to you.

MATTHEW 4:18-22

Jesus died and rose,
for me and for you.

MATTHEW 21:1-11, 26:17-50, 27:32-54, 28

Children, children,
what is true?

Jesus is a gift,
for me and for you.

JOHN 3:16